MYSTERIES

OF

BLACK HOLES
AND
DARK MATTER

by Ellen Labrecque

CAPSTONE PRESS
a capstone imprint

Capstone Captivate is published by Capstone Press, an imprint of Capstone.
1710 Roe Crest Drive
North Mankato, Minnesota 56003
www.capstonepub.com

Library of Congress Cataloging-in-Publication Data
Library of Congress Cataloging-in-Publication Data is available on the Library of Congress website.

ISBN: 978-1-4966-8075-4 (library binding)
ISBN: 978-1-4966-8715-9 (paperback)
ISBN: 978-1-4966-8169-0 (eBook PDF)

Summary: What is a black hole? What is dark matter and what is it made of? How do scientists discover black holes and dark matter if they can't be seen? What do scientists know about these mysterious parts of the universe and what do they still hope to find out? Budding astronomers will learn the answers to these questions and more!

Image Credits
Alamy: TCD/Prod.DB, 28; Getty Images: National Science Foundation, 11; NASA: ESA, S. Beckwith (STScI) and the HUDF Team, 27, X-ray: NASA/CXC/CfA/M.Markevitch et al., Optical: NASA/STScI, Magellan/U.Arizona/D.Clowe et al., Lensing Map: NASA/STScI, ESO WFI, Magellan/U.Arizona/D.Clowe et al., 22; Newscom: World History Archive/NASA, ESA, and The Hubble Heritage Team, 19; Science Source: American Institute of Physics/Emilio Segrè Visual Archives, 13, ESO/APEX/2MASS/Andreas Eckart et al./Luís Calçada, 16, Jerry Lodriguss, 20–21, Mikkel Juul Jensen, 6–7; Shutterstock: Allexxandar, 7, artjazz, 29, Dominate Studio, 5, Marc Ward, 15, Nasky, 26, rkafoto, 10, u3d, 8, VectorMine, 21, 25; Wikimedia: Sloan Digital Sky Survey, 9, Unknown photographer, 12

Design Elements
Shutterstock: Anna Kutukova, Aygun Ali

Editorial Credits
Editor: Hank Musolf; Designer: Sara Radka; Media Researcher: Jo Miller; Production Specialist: Laura Manthe

All internet sites appearing in back matter were available and accurate when this book was sent to press.

TABLE OF CONTENTS

Words in **bold** are in the glossary.

CHAPTER 1

WHAT ARE BLACK HOLES?

Black holes are one of the most mysterious things in the universe. For many years, **astronomers** weren't sure if black holes were real. They couldn't see them. Yet they suspected they were there. Black holes do things to **matter** around them. They pull in anything that gets near them. They are very powerful. They even swallow up light! Black holes also slow down time. They stretch out in space. It wasn't until 1994 that scientists finally proved that they exist. But there are still things that scientists are still trying to learn about them.

The universe is filled with mysteries like black holes. Another mystery is dark matter. There is still much to learn about this invisible substance in space. Scientists work every day to try to solve these mysteries and more.

MYSTERY FACT

There are too many black holes in outer space to count.

It took many years for scientists to prove that black holes were real.

The formation of a black hole

a star collapses and dies

the core of the star remains

Black holes are stars that have died and collapsed in on themselves. Stars live for more than 10 billion years. When a giant star finally dies, it explodes. This explosion is called a **supernova**. It only lasts about 100 seconds. The outer bits of the star fly off into space. The center, or **core** of the star, remains. **Gravity** squeezes the core. A black hole is born.

MYSTERY FACT

Astronomers think a supernova will be visible from Earth from a telescope over the next 50 years.

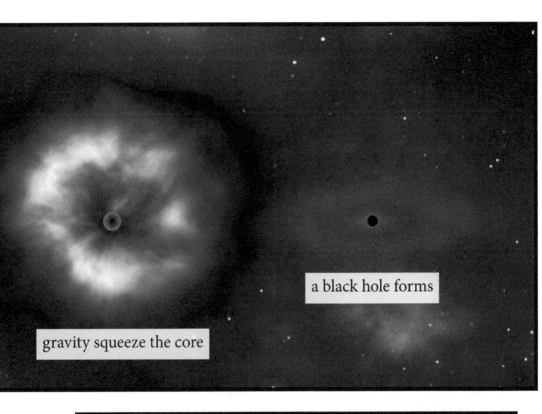

gravity squeeze the core

a black hole forms

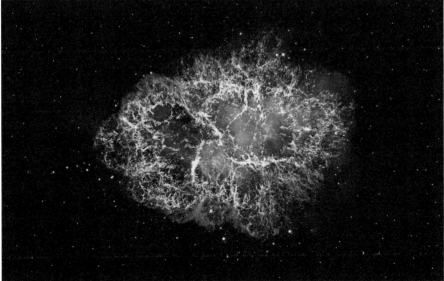

Part of a supernova in the constellation of Taurus

A black hole attracts space matter.

Black holes are not empty space. In fact, they are stuffed tightly with matter. This makes black holes very heavy. The heavier something is, the more gravity it has. The more gravity something has, the stronger the pull it has. Black holes are heavier and have more pull than anything else in the universe. If a light was shining right next to a black hole, we would not see it. Instead, the black hole would swallow it up!

LIGHT-YEARS

The closest black hole to Earth is 3,000 light-years away! A light-year is the distance that light travels in one year. We use light-years to measure distance in space. One light-year is equal to about 5.88 trillion miles (9.46 trillion kilometers).

CHAPTER 2

BLACK HOLE DISCOVERY

Scientists can't see black holes. Yet they know they are there. How? They affect the objects around them. Before matter is pulled into the black hole, it swirls around it. Imagine water going down the drain in a sink. It goes around the drain before going into it. It is the same way with black holes. When black holes pull objects in, the area around them gets super hot. This is because of **friction** of gas particles around the black hole. This high heat gives off **x-rays**. X-rays are waves of energy. Scientists can detect these waves of energy.

Matter being pulled into a black hole is similar to water going down a drain.

In April 2019, the first photo of activity around a black hole was released. It is outlined by the hot gas swirling around it, which is being pulled by gravity.

ALBERT EINSTEIN'S DISCOVERIES

Albert Einstein is one of the most famous scientists who ever lived. He was born in 1879 in Germany. He studied science all his life. His discoveries changed the way we think about time, space, and matter. Recent research about black holes not only has confirmed the existence of black holes, but has further confirmed many of his discoveries about space.

John Wheeler was one of the first scientists to study theories of black holes.

In 1915, Albert Einstein was the first scientist to believe that black holes were possible. He understood that empty, dark space doesn't mean that nothing is there. Einstein came up with a theory: If gravity became strong enough, it could rob light of all its energy. Gravity could trap the light forever. In 1967, American scientist John Wheeler named these dark areas black holes.

CHAPTER 3

BLACK HOLE TYPES

Earth is in the Milky Way Galaxy. In our galaxy alone, there could be a billion black holes!

Sometimes black holes come together to become one massive black hole. When two black holes merge, they create a gravity wave. A gravity wave is like an earthquake in space. It is a fast and invisible ripple in the universe. In 2015, using high-tech equipment, scientists heard a gravity wave when two black holes collided.

MYSTERY FACT

There is a huge black hole at the center of the Milky Way Galaxy. It is named Sagittarius A.

A black hole pulls in gas and dust.

Sagittarius A*

Sgr A* is a supermassive black hole in the center of the Milky Way Galaxy.

There are three different types of black holes. They are stellar black holes, supermassive black holes, and intermediate black holes. Stellar black holes are the smallest type of black hole. They have five to ten times the **mass** of our sun. They are the most common type in our universe. Stellar black holes continue to grow. They pull in the dust and the gas surrounding them.

Supermassive black holes are much bigger. They can be a billion times bigger than our sun. Scientists believe they formed from smaller black holes smashing together. Supermassive black holes lie at the center of every galaxy.

Intermediate black holes are the third kind. They are medium-sized. Scientists believed for a long time only big and small black holes existed. In 2014, they discovered intermediate ones too.

CHAPTER 4

DARK MATTER

Dark matter is even more mysterious than black holes. Dark matter is an invisible substance. It clumps together due to gravity. It does not **absorb**, **reflect**, or give off light. It makes up 80 percent of our universe. Astronomers suspect that dark matter surrounds all the galaxies. It keeps them together. Without dark matter, galaxies might fly apart. Scientists can't see dark matter. Like with black holes, they have had to figure out different ways to prove it exists. A few scientists still question the existence of dark matter, but most studies show that dark matter does exist.

A ring of dark matter surrounds a group of galaxies. Dark matter cannot be seen, but it can be located by studying the appearance of space around it.

IC 3476
IC 3523
IC 3575
IC 3567
IC 3520
4506
IC 3501
IC 3583
M90
4531
IC 3486
IC 3492
IC3475
IC 3540
IC 3506
IC 3457

Galaxies are clustered in space because of dark matter. Our Milky Way Galaxy is part of the Virgo Supercluster. Dark matter keeps galaxies together. It can also bend light. Light from a distant galaxy will bend. It will go around dark matter in different directions. This makes it seem like there is more than one light source. But there isn't. This bending of light is called **gravitational lensing**. It is one way for scientists to prove the existence of dark matter.

4474
4468
4459
4446

The Virgo cluster of galaxies

4477
4479
IC 3382
4473
IC 3280
4458
IC 3386   IC 3355
4461
4402
4435
4438
IC 3393   M86
IC 3388   M84
4387
IC 3303
4425
4388
4413

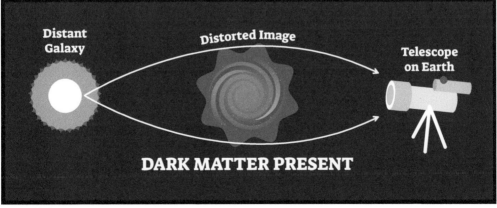

Dark matter is found by locating places in space where light
is bent or distorted.

Two pink clumps of hot gas show a collision between two galaxies. Scientists believe dark matter is in the blue areas.

In 2006, two large cluster galaxies collided together. Scientists were able to observe this crash through powerful telescopes. The crash was mighty. Regular matter and dark matter were ripped apart. Regular matter was stripped away. Two clumps of dark matter were left behind. Scientists knew it was dark matter because of the way it was acting with light. Before this crash, some scientists didn't think dark matter existed. Once this crash happened, more scientists began to believe it did.

CHAPTER 5

DARK ENERGY

Our universe is expanding. Galaxies that are far from us are only moving farther away. Scientists still don't understand why. Some theories state that another mysterious force in space called dark energy is the cause. This is a type of energy we can't see. We still know it is there.

Scientists think this dark energy is like a fluid that is just flying around in space. Dark energy is the exact opposite of gravity. It is anti-gravity. While dark matter holds everything together, dark energy pulls everything apart.

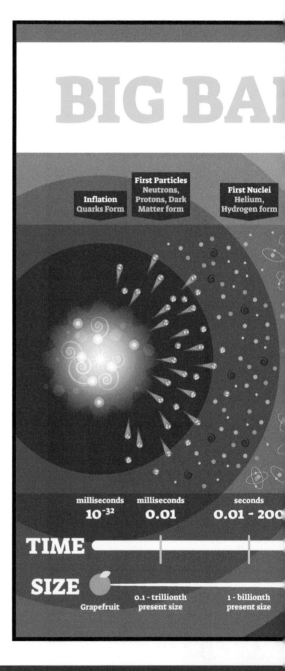

BIG BA|

Inflation
Quarks Form

First Particles
Neutrons,
Protons, Dark
Matter form

First Nuclei
Helium,
Hydrogen form

| milliseconds 10^{-32} | milliseconds 0.01 | seconds 0.01 - 200 |

TIME

SIZE

Grapefruit

0.1 - trillionth
present size

1 - billionth
present size

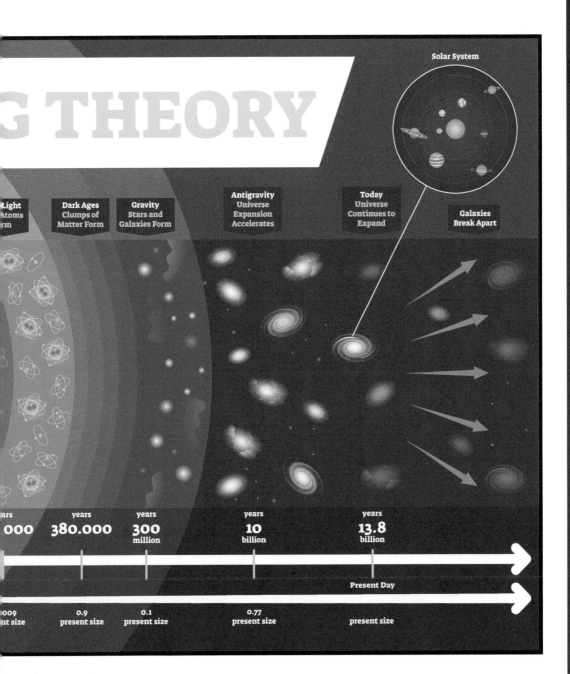

G THEORY

Solar System

| Light
Atoms
rm | Dark Ages
Clumps of
Matter Form | Gravity
Stars and
Galaxies Form | Antigravity
Universe
Expansion
Accelerates | Today
Universe
Continues to
Expand | Galaxies
Break Apart |

ars	years	years	years	years	
000	**380.000**	**300** million	**10** billion	**13.8** billion	

Present Day

| 009
nt size | 0.9
present size | 0.1
present size | 0.77
present size | present size |

CHAPTER 6

SO MUCH STILL TO LEARN

Only about 5 percent of the universe is made up of things we can see, such as galaxies, stars, and light. All the things we can't see, such as dark matter and dark energy, make up just more than 95 percent.

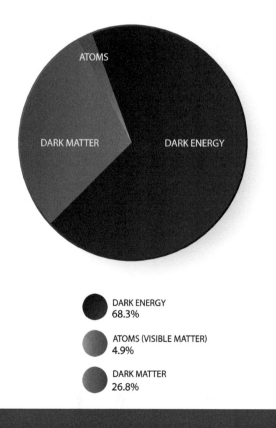

ATOMS

DARK MATTER

DARK ENERGY

DARK ENERGY
68.3%

ATOMS (VISIBLE MATTER)
4.9%

DARK MATTER
26.8%

Stars are made of visible matter, so we can see them.

Scientists are discovering more and more about this 95 percent. Yet the universe still holds many secrets. Scientists know that black holes, dark matter, and dark energy all exist. But they don't know why. They don't know what exactly makes up dark matter. They don't know exactly what happens inside a black hole. Some scientists believe that we can travel through time in a black hole. Others believe everything just burns up once inside.

MYSTERY FACT

The movie *Interstellar* is about a father who travels in time through black holes.

Scientists are working hard to find answers. Astronomers are measuring the x-rays of different kinds of black holes. They are using new technology to try to detect dark matter and dark energy.

We are just beginning to understand the mysteries of space. But with each new discovery scientists make, they are one step closer to solving the many mysteries of the universe.

GLOSSARY

absorb (ab-ZORB)—to take something in

astronomer (uh-STRON-uh-mer)—someone who studies outer space

core (KOHR)—the central or innermost part of something

friction (FRIK-shun)—the rubbing of the surface of one body to another

gravitational lensing (grav-i-TEY-shun-ul; lenz-ing)—bending of light from a distant source

gravity (GRAV-i-tee)—the force of attraction by which a smaller object is pulled toward the center of a larger object

mass (MAS)—a body of matter

matter (MAT-er)—anything that occupies space

reflect (ri-FLEKT)—to bounce off an object

supernova (soo-per-NOH-va)—the violent and bright explosion at the end of a star's life

x-ray (EKS-rey)—a form of radiation; similar to light but a shorter wavelength

READ MORE

Coppens, Katie, and Grant Tremblay. *What Do Black Holes Eat for Dinner?* Boston, MA: Tumblehome Learning Inc., 2020.

Gifford, Clive. *Super Space Encyclopedia.* New York: DK Publishing, 2019.

Orr, Tamra. *Space Discoveries.* North Mankato, MN: Capstone Press, 2019.

INTERNET SITES

Hubble Space Telescope: Black Holes
https://hubblesite.org/contents/articles/black-holes.html

NASA: Black Holes
https://science.nasa.gov/astrophysics/focus-areas/black-holes/

National Science Foundation: Black Holes
https://www.nsf.gov/news/special_reports/blackholes/

INDEX